In Deep, Deep Waters of Hurricane Katrina:

In Deep, Deep Waters of Hurricane Katrina:

The Aftermath Untold Stories

Cheryl Richardson

To order additional copies of this book, contact:
Xlibris Corporation
1-888-795-4274
www.Xlibris.com
Orders@Xlibris.com
60025

Dedication

This book is written by
Cheryl Richardson and dedicated to my husband, Edward Richardson.

His leadership has restored our family through prayers,
patience and forgiveness.
God has granted us a new life and a new way of living.
We appreciate God's love and his Grace.

Introduction

This is a true story about the Hurricane Katrina's wild gusty winds and floodwaters that almost wiped out our neighborhood and the residences that were in its path.

We all witnessed nature's fury at its worst and all of its destruction. The memories will never abort our minds.

Chapter 1

In Deep Deep Waters of
Hurricane Katrina
The Aftermath
Untold Stories

It was a beautiful Sunday afternoon when the weatherman announce that the storm call Hurricane Katrina are in route, and maybe heading to the Gulf Port Area, invading the city of New Orleans. He asked the people to prepare themselves for the four category storm, by escaping from out of the city. Our neighborhood resident & others became afraid from hearing the newscaster warning. My husband who name is Edward listen intensity to any changes in the huge hurricane status. I walk outdoor to witness the clouds fierceness. There is none. The sun is shining bright. Many of people are loading their vehicles to leave. The family that resided across the street has abandoned their upstairs home. My nearest neighbors alone with friends are barbecuing on their grill. I am witnessing everyone activities. My telephone rang. Edward answered the call. He shout for me to come inside to talk on the line. The caller is my youngest son name Darell. He is away at college, and has been inform about the monstrous upcoming Hurricane Katrina and the devastation that it will bring. He wanted to know our plan for exit. I sadly express to him, that Edward and I have a financial shortage. We had recently paid, household bills. Darell suggest that we walk down the street to the next corner from our house and get on the bus that are loading people to take them to a evacuation site. He was very concern about our safety. We agreed to check things out. We walk towards the school where the buses are parked. Eddie & I discuss our options. We discover that there is no charge for the ride. The bus driver advised us that the destination site is the Superdome. Our main concern is our finances. We have very little money. We decided to stay home. A lot of our neighbors decide to stay behind too. Eddie & I were thankful that Darell was away at college in Alabama. All of the neighborhood kids had gone away. Two days before we know anything about the arrival of Hurricane Katrina. I had called the SPCA to shelter Darell's dog who name is Nite. I was no longer able to care for him because he was huge & strong. We found him another home. Eddie had never been in a hurricane before. He was frightened of the unknown possibilities. I am familiar with the effect of major hurricanes. I have to coach him, and pray that Hurricane Katrina will downgrade to heavy rain & light winds. Family members are concern for themselves, us and other people of the community. The realization is that people stay behind because of their finances and other issues. I know that people desire to leave their areas. When Katrina approached, our prayers were more intense. Eddie & I put our safety plans in motion. We took all of the pictures off the wall and store them in boxes. I place my son's ceramics in-between the dresser & gather our important papers and place them in a plastic bag. I told Eddie to place our 7ft. ladder in the living room area near the front door. He reminded me to place my medications, I.D. picture and eyeglasses nearby. We laid our clothes and shoes next to the bed in reachable sight. Afterwards, we laid quietly when the drama began. We heard the howling gusty winds, heavy rain down pours, banging against the aluminum siding hitting the house ripping and tearing off the boards. Flood waters was forcing the back door open. The large tree that stood between my nearest neighbor's house and ours was banging it limbs & branches heavily on the rooftop. Wild winds knocked out many of the window panes. The whistling winds were horrifying. Eddie looked at me with disbelief. I suggest that we get out of bed on to the floor and pray. We did. Soon the telephone rang. We are to frighten to move out of our position to answer the ringing. It stopped and shut itself off. The lights flicker on and off, into darkness in the front area. Our decision to stay home seemed foolish now. The storm worsened. Our son had warned us to get out. Eddie & I continue to kneel in prayer. I look toward the back door entrance. The kitchen ceiling caved in. The flood waters push the wash machine dryer, stove, kitchen table and chairs through several rooms in our directions. We panic. Eddie shouted for me to get fully dress, soon we heard banging on the walls. It is our neighbors informing us,

on how high the water is outdoors. It was well over the height of the mailbox
and still rising. The men search for the attic using a shovel and a crowbar.
They found its location. Eddie place the ladder underneath the round hold
they had made. He climbed up the ladder into the attic first. We were aware
of the unwelcome guest that resided in there. We share the space with small
birds, pigeons and the rats. It was six twenty Monday morning when all of
us neighbors climb up. We prayed for our safety and for the weather to calm
down. The wild winds and heavy raindrops had no mercy as the water rose
higher and higher underneath of our feet. The hard rain tore the back rooftop
off the house. We huddle together for protection. We scream loudly for God
to help us survive this destruction. In the midst of catastrophe, we discuss
how devastate, and unforgiving our children will be if we do not make it
out this attic alive. Tracy, Darell's girlfriend had given birth to their first
baby. I thought about their safety as well. I prayed that the rest of my family
has made it out of the storm or even out the city alive and safely. Soon the
water level remained at a stand still. We began making plans to escape. We
didn't want night time to catch us still there or come in contact with any
rodents. We form a line. I stepped to the side to make space for everyone
to come down on the ladder. I placed my feet on the sheet rock. Suddenly,
I dropped down straight into the cold muddy water. Everyone heard the
big splash as the deep, deep water consume me. I heard Eddie scream out
my name in fear as he was watching me drowning. The more I tried to stay
on top of the water, the more it surrounded and pulled me underneath. I
struggle at the bottom, bubbles was forming. I began having a conversation
with God. I told him that I am not ready to leave this world yet. I beg him
for more time. Then I heard another big splash and realizes that it is Eddie.
He jumped into the deep deep cold, muddy water to rescue me. I felt him
pull me by the collar of my shirt. Another guy jumped into the water. He
was trying to pull the door open for Eddie & I to get through. The harder
he pull the door. The violent water beat against it and made it hard to open.
Eddie & I were cold and trembling. We could not swim in that high amount
of water. The guy finally was able to get the door unjammed. We went inside
our house onto the 7ft ladder. Eddie was checking my body for injuries. I
had scrapes & cuts, but I was mostly scared and freezing cold. Eddie
announced to me that we most go back up into the attic. I scream out no
way!" I am not going back up there. He convinced me that if we do not go,
we will drown in our house on this ladder. He warned me to stay on the
beam this time. Eddie assist me back up there I sat down on the beam and
crossed my legs. I stayed in the position for hours, until the guys concocted

a plan for all of us to try a escape attempt again. The men went into the deep waters first, entering into the houses gathering sheets, blankets, bed spreads, cords, tape, rope & string. They tied those items together using them as grips for each individual to hold on to so no one would be dragged underneath the deep, deep waters. The ladies heard the guys planning and discussing their options as they look out from the window. I was getting stiff from sitting on the beam. I finally found the nerve to get up and walk to the nearby window to witness the activity of the hurricane wild gusty winds & high flood water. The fellows were swimming across in the water to get to the other side of the street where the higher house was located. We watch in horror, screaming for the men to be careful. The women witness them breaking the window panes and entering into the house. They began assembling the materials, mixing the long cords, string & rope together making it long and strong. The guys dip in and out of the water gathering lumber wood, that was flowing down stream. There were big sticks, to make a raft. It stood on top of the water and was able to hold three people on it at a time. The men pull the raft from one end of the street across to the other side. The elderly folks got on board first. The folks were pulled across on the raft in the violent, blowing winds and heavy rainfall down pours beat on them. Soon it was the ladies turn to board. I sat directly in the middle of the raft for balance so that we didn't tilt over. We were understandable afraid. None of us females could swim. We coach each other to remain calm as the rain continued to abuse our body. After everyone had made it across without drowning there were a large Rottweiler dog a German shepherd dog and kitten we rescue. The animals did not panic, although they were afraid but remain humble. We were cold, wet and shaking. The guys tied the raft and cords to the rails of the nearby stairs. The water continued to abuse our city and the residence that stay behind. The raft held our weight and kept us from sinking. The fifteen of us enter our neighbor's house, searching for dry towels, food and clean water to drink. We opened the food pantry and refrigerator door. We witness food in there. I was appointed the chef. I declined. I explain that I am hurt from the fall but Eddie insisted that I move around so my body would not stiffer. I agreed to be the cook. I ask for assisted in preparing the food. We all ate, than everyone claim a sleeping spot. The bedroom or sofa. Eddie and I had a private room to nurse my injuries. When night came, we searched for candles, drank liquor and we all took sleeping pills. We were so shaken and needed to relax. We gather outdoors on the porch through the darkness, the thousand of stars gave us its lights. Everything was quite and still. We stared into the black dirty water.

I look into it with anger, realizing that the water try to consume my life without warning.

Someone started telling silly jokes by candlelight I joined in. We allowed ourselves to laugh to keep from crying. We got strength from one another. No one wanted to think about the long road ahead to recovery. We were enjoying the moment. The airplanes and helicopter continue to fly over and around our setting. We would stop talking and start shouting flaging for rescue to help us and notice that we are stranded. The air chopper couldn't make it in-between the power lines. The water was still rising even though we were high off the ground. I look directly across the street at our house. It was flooded out. The ceiling and roof were off. I thought about losing all of the contents and our personal stuff inside. My son's ashes were in there. His ceramics was heavy. I couldn't carry them out. I became sadden. My son ashes are burial after all.

The only property that Eddie could save is the Holy Bible that laid on the end table near the doorway. Three days later the gas and water in the higher house was cut off. We had to execute and exit plans and our fear of the deep, deep waters was going to be our greatest challenge. We scoop, wood, lumber and small sticks out of the unclean water. The guys made long length rafts with the wood boards. They made three of them to load five people on each one. We boarded on the rafts with luggage that we had taken from the house and the rescue animals boarded also. The men stirred the long stick front and back into the water for guidance. The ladies place their small sticks into the water to help the raft movement. It took us three hours of travel on the raft to do what would have taken a ten minutes walk down the street to the corners. We separated when we reach dry land. Everyone wish each other good luck as we journey to our unknown destination. Eddie & I headed for walking through the French Quarter a short cut to Canal Street. People told us that we must go to the Convention Center. The Superdome was filled to capacity with the city folks evacuees. The days that we spent in the house. We lost a lot of precious hours. We miss the evacuation plans. Each street corner that Eddie & I walked on

Chapter 2

I had to stop for a few minutes. I was having hard stomach pains. It was nightime when we arrived near the Convention Center. We stop in the Hilton Hotel parking garage lot area. We camp outside on the curb side near a Mexican's family. We lay on the concrete ground. Eddie told the family members that his wife is injured and we are very tired. We use our luggage for a pillow. We woke up early morning to loud talking. There are thousands & thousands of people roaming around in the street. We were only one block from the Convention Center. The people were asking each other questions. No one had answers. The crowd had been living on the streets for four days waiting for the buses, ships, airplanes & trains transportation to remove them out of the city. New Orleans look doom. The heat index is 103° degrees. I place a towel over my head & continually poured water on it to keep cool. I felt faint. There is a lot of elderly, wheelchair bound, new born babies young children, sick folks, disease infective & mental ill among the would he healthy people. Everyone is breathing in toxic air there is a tall building that surround near us is burning down to the ground without water assistance. As time went on, the people started to argue and demanded answers from the Governor, Mayor, Councilmen, Senators & the President of the United States by the news cameras, media. They ask them to have & display compassion & empathy for our plight. The newscaster was assisting us in getting attention. Many people were crying because they want to leave out of the city. Others are crying because they didn't want to leave from their home. The Police Department was treating this situation as a local crisis. They were emotional and upset themselves. They abandon the people later on so they can go and check on their families and assess their own damages, or act on whatever could be salvage. Our Police Officers was not train for this magnitude of tragedy. The citizens witness their productivity. The Military Force were call in to maintain order and protection. They made a Headquarter in the site on the ground. They distribute food and water to each individual. The soldiers monitor the single form line. The elderly, handicap, young children and sick folks were served their meals first than the other folks. After eating, the crowd of people settled down. The Military Police banish their weapons at all times. They still display human sympathy for the American's People. Their mission is to maintain order. I ask a Solider does he know when the transportation will arrive? He answered me back, saying. We are under strict orders not to discuss that. I shook my head in despair. I am afraid when nighttime comes. We are still sleeping on the concrete in the streets. The airplane & choppers flew all day in the city with a watchful eye. They couldn't control the darkness and its danger &

conflicts among the crowd. There are so many honest & innocent people out there, trying to cope in this unfamiliar territory.

When nighttime is unto us, there was darkness without lighting the moon gives out its radiate. As quietness settle in, I can hear people crying, praying & checking on their young children. Everyone is vulnerable, as we lay down on the concrete ground. I began to breakdown in tears. I am overwhelmed. It seems as though the world had come to an end, we are the only survivors. The military police couldn't control the hours or actions. There were sexual predators, roaming in the darkness looking for prey. They are raping & sexual assaulting females. The bad elements of men had no mercy on their victims. I heard screaming from across the streets area. The mischievous males, enjoyed breaking into stores hotels, restaurants & bar lounges. The Military Police couldn't watch all of the activities that were going on. When morning came, thousands of impatience folks started arguing, fighting & threatening the police into battle. Other people are frustrated from witnessing their love ones dying because they couldn't hold on to life anymore waiting for the buses to arrive. Young thugs will shoot their guns, while hiding in the crowds parents are gathering their babies closer to them for protection & safety. It is exactly four days that Eddie & I joined the folks. Eddie walked closer to the Convention Center to hear information about when the buses are coming to rescue us out of the violent city. The updated news is that the buses are in route, form a single line. No one can take any pets on the buses.

The pet owners became enraged by screaming and yelling at the bus driver to allow their pets to board the bus. Their behavior slow the process of the people need to get on the bus. We were sitting on the sidewalk curb drinking liquor and talking loudly to entertain each other until we got closer to the bus. The police assist the elderly, handicap, wheelchair bound, infants, and young children on first. When the last bus was filling up, the driver announced that there were two seats left. The crowd pushed Eddie & I towards the front line, because we were a couple and I seem injured. We thank them as we board. There were so many family members that has gotten separate. Husbands couldn't find their wives, mothers lost their children in the crowd. After we board on the cool and soft chairs, Eddie & I were relieved. We know that tonight, we won't be sleeping outdoors in darkness or on the pavement. I have sorrow in my heart for the thousands of folks that were left behind. There should be one hundred, and fifty more buses in route to retrieve the other folks. Eddie & I bonded with the Mexican's family that laid on the ground near us. I ask them if they're leaving the city also. They said no. They will stay behind for employment. The bus driver drove all day & night. The people are asleep. Later on I read a sign stating Welcome to the State of Texas. The bus driver pulled into a park, picnic area, where there are long tables, ice coolers, plenty of food & personal items on them. The driver told the people to get off the bus to eat & drink. Take any amount of personal items we need for a long travel.

There were friendly looking faces that stood near the tables to greet us the ladies allow us to use their cell phones to contact our families' long distant relatives to let them know that we are out of our city. Later that night we board the bus again. Most of the folks went to sleep on the long ride to an undisclosed location. It was early sunrise when the bus driver park at the curb. The sign read Welcome to the State of Arkansas. Folks woke up from their sleep, fussing & cursing to the driver. They said to him. We did not authorize coming this far away from our home town. The driver told the people to get off the bus once again. This is our evacuation site. I stepped off. I saw a few people that I am familiar with. I ask them, did they see my sisters, nieces, nephews, Tracy & my new born grandbaby? Someone respond saying yes. They were in the Superdome heading to the state of Texas by airplane. Eddie & I are on a military base. Soon, the one hundred & fifty more buses parked near the curb. There are three hundred buses out here. This compound site has plenty of land, dirt, ground, apartment, housing, barracks and open field area.

The soldiers brandish their guns to show authority & protection of this site. They search the buses looking for drugs & weapons. They are digging into the folks luggages without their permission. The people got angry. Since we are at our destination, I decided to check out my injures by medical services. They are on the grounds. I walked up to the Red Cross Center. I ask a nurse to check my vital signs. She did. I am informed that my sugar level is very high out of range. My blood pressure is extremely up. I am told that their facilities are equipped to offer me a ride to the local hospital in an ambulance. Eddie told the nurse that he must come alone. He didn't want us to get separated. They agreed to keep me at the site until he goes to the bus to get our luggage and our belonging that we left on the seat. When he return back to medical, I am taken to the local hospital for treatment. The nurse place me in a single room. The doctor began working on my situation. The door open & close from staff employees entering with concern. They are watching the television news on a cable station, having plenty of sympathy for the residence of the Gulf port area. Eddie washed off the heavy dust from his clothing. The nurse offered him a tray of food. The victims of Hurricane Katrina were begging the government for assistance. There are many other people who has been left behind. I began to cry. The program on television is real. Home for the citizens would never be as we once knew it to be. We lost everything that's materialism. Hurricane Katrina tried to take our life. We fought back with unity, we survived. We paddle and stirred out. My potassium is low from the days of living in the street. I am treated and released. The military soldiers drove Eddie & I back to their barracks in a jeep. We were assign single beds. We place ours together and settle into the sleeping quarters. We were tired. I had a lot of medications inside my body, enough for more traveling. The next evening the military police came into the dormitory to announce that we have to pack up and leave out again immediately. He explained that the people who are in this location must be transfer to another site. This part of the dormitory cannot be monitor or protected. There isn't enough soldiers. Our next evacuation site will be in another city of Arkansas. Eddie & I board the bus again at one o'clock p.m. The bus driver drove all day long. The highway is narrow, the curbs and turn are sharp. I kept praying for this nightmare to end. I watch out the window witness the beautiful scenery and God's creations were breath taking. This was my only solace. I am appreciating being alive. Late into the evening the bus driver pulled into a lot.

The sign read Christian Retreat. This area is a camp site in the woods off the highway. Many people approach the bus in an effort to assist us with our needs.

They sympathized with our plight and reassure us that we are saved. We were asked to stand in a line to take I.D. pictures & thumb print. We were assign cabin housing. In this area there are hills, small mountains, gravel rocks and dirt. The lady assigned, Eddie & I a cabin on the hilltop. He had to pull me up by my hands I am hurting again. The medication has wore off. We hike up there. I kept watching my step, looking down for spiders, crickets, snails bugs and insects. We enter into the lodge. There are no locks on the door. This unit is very large. I demand Eddie to place the kitchen table in front of the door. There are nine bulk beds stack on top of one another, almost touching the ceiling. I ask him to place two beds together making one king size one. I pleaded with him to leave the bathroom light on. We laid in bed. I thought of all the creepy insects indoors and the wild life animals outdoors such as, bears, deer, wolves and frogs. We conversed before he went to sleep. Early morning I open the door to witness the heavy fog throughout the trees. The scenery from the hill is beautiful. As a child I wanted to spend one night in a log cabin. This time wasn't right. I enter into the shower. I watch the water stream from its pipe with fear. Eddie & I went to breakfast in the diner. All of the people are struggling to communicate with the camp site employees. The only person who we need to talk to is Fema (Federal Government Agency) someone ask the question has Fema been notified of our whereabouts? The camp employee answered yes. They will come to this site at noon today. A truck pulled up. There are ten men in uniforms with the name Fema located on their shirt. They jump off of the trucks onto the dusty ground. Boldly telling the folks that this organization isn't prepared to assist them at this time. Folks has to be at a stable location, have a telephone number, proof of the location of the disaster area location. The people screamed at Fema asking them for assets to the use of computers & cell phones? They ask the men. Why did that come out to this site with disappointing news. Family members huddle together saying. We must spend another night in the cabins. The tears stream down their face. Seven days ago Hurricane Katrina hit our city, we are still traveling on the road deeper into exile. There are no solutions for the people in this aftermath. It's one hundred, twenty five people in this group. We are frustrated. The facts is, these folks has lost their residence and all of its contents. Of course they are in despair. Eddie & I hiked up to our assigned cabin room. I'm at a loss for words, and I began to cry. He assured me that this will be our last night there in the woods. He will call Darell on the telephone in the morning to let him know that we are alright here in Arkansas.

Eddie telephoned his dad. His wife answer the phone with much concern she said dad isn't in. Eddie told her, he'll call back later. When nighttime came, he called his dad back. He asked him to telephone Darell at the college. Tell him that we are still traveling, we haven't settle down in one location yet. Tell him to stand near the telephone booth and wait for our telephone call. The next day Eddie telephone Darell, before he started his classes. He re-assured him that we are alright. He reach me the telephone. I talked to my son. He could hardly understand my words I tremble from all of the excitement I couldn't contain my nerves. I ask him, had he heard from Tracy and how is their baby? Darell said he talked to her, Darielle is fine. They are in the state of Texas. He ask me to put Eddie back on the telephone line? Darell told Eddie that he talked to his faculty members at the college. He asked them, can they put his parents in an apartment out of harm's way? The dean agreed to that idea. She said if we can make it to Birmingham, they will assist us. It is confirmed to be true. Eddie told the camp site sponsor lady, that we have made contact with the people in the state of Alabama, where our son attends school. She gave us money and a one way bus ticket. We boarded on Greyhound bus. We rode a whole day, we arrived here at the bus station on Friday evening. Eddie telephoned the dean stating that we have arrived.

Chapter 3

A faculty member from the college met us at the bus station. He is a very nice man & is concern about the events that is happening abode. We arrived at the campus to meet the two ladies deans. They escorted us to the diner for meals. We met the athletic coach. He brought us to the apartments to settle in. Later that night about ten thirty p.m. I heard a knock on the door. It is the coach, with Darell. He is a sight for sore eyes. We embrace, I witness the worried expression on his face. I look like I had been through pure hell. Eddie told Darell that we lost all of our contexts. He was only able to retrieve our family Bible that laid on the table near the door. He also said that his brother who name is George want us to travel up north, because Fema is helping families there. Eddie declined saying that your mother need to come near you. After a few days of settling in, I am experiencing sudden body chills and I have a high fever. My husband telephone an ambulance, I was treated for phenomenon & later released with medications. One day I sat outdoors for fresh air. The athletic coach passed by. He said you seem to be in deep thought. I respond saying yes. He said "count it all joy that you & your family made it out. I was trying to understand that lodge. Home for us will never be as we knew & left it. The city would need major construction. The only property that is still standing strong is the seven ft ladder. A reminder of Hurricane Katrina & Rita. My sister Cynthia had finally located our mother in a Nursing Hospital Unit. Her name is Nancy. She was evacuate by helicopter to a small country town. I was relieved to know that she was hustle away from the city that she loved and witnessed its destruction. Mother is discharge from the residence place. It was Saturday evening when my sister who name is Cynthia & Mr. Joe who is my step father. Nikki & Syeshia my nieces went there to take her home to Baton Rouge Louisiana. They cannot reunite mother with her other children. She is happy leaving with them. I am sure that she is enjoying the long car ride and witnessing the beautiful country scenery. She like the outdoor and is a little weak. Her leaving the facilities was against medical advice. It was her decision. They couldn't hold her against her will. She has a strong desire to be with her family. I can remember a conversation, Mama & I had when I spoke to her on the telephone. She was sharing with me about her evacuation. It was her first airplane ride. I ask her was she afraid? She answered no. She really enjoyed it. The nurses & doctors were very attentive to her need. She was happy to ride out by first class. We laugh at that situation. I was please to hear her voice, so was she to hear mines. Even though we had uncertainties about the future. They arrived to Baton Rouge safely and settle our mother comfortably for the night. I telephone her early Sunday morning, she pick up the phone line and said hello in her natural high pitch voice. As I began to ask mama a question, I could hear her struggling to answer I end our conversation. After I hang up, I became very concern & upset. Eddie offer to take me shopping to relieve me from my negative thoughts & sorrows. When we return to the apartments Darell appear. I greeted him with saying hello. He answer me back in a whisper sound. I ask him what his problem was. He told me to sat down. I did. He responded saying your mother has died. I scream loudly, saying that she can't leave us now. We need her strength, support & encouragement. I believe that the stress of Hurricane Katrina had weight heavily on her heart & mind. The news media is continuing to show so much water damage & flooding. Mama knew that it would be years before she can return home. I cried hard tears when I thought of how unhappy & lost she may have felt. My only solace was, the fact that she was aware that her family was save and out the abandon city. Eddie & I was still tired from all of those days on the highway through our evacuation plans.

It was a must that we get on the highway again heading to Baton Rough. Eddie, Darell, Tracy and their baby, myself and Andrew Darell's college roommate exit out of Birmingham.

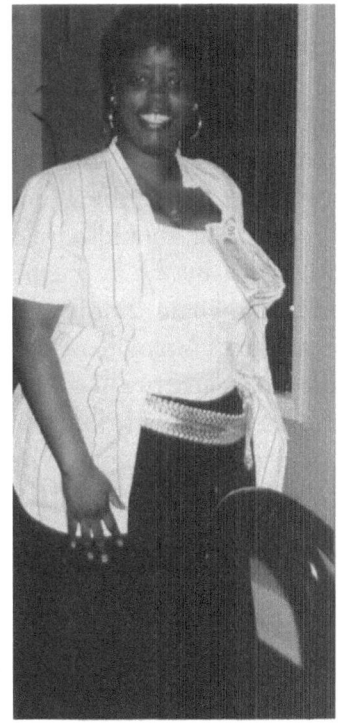

We lived at my sister's house for a week. We have seen Mr. Joe once again since the storm. Everyone made a strong effort to be strong and laid our dear mother out nicely in her untimely death. Family members came from different states. Her services were emotional & confusing. All of us is going to have a empty space without Nancy. She was generally one of a kind. Our best buddy, a teenage mom, who was devoted to her children. I believe that she favor my sisters more than I. We talked about our situation. She explain, that I was always going away to explore life. My sisters were dedicated to her. It was my fault that I am adventurous and miss out on her nurturing. My personal thought about home is. It will always be there when I return. She should have not held that against me. I felt her resentment & outcast by family members. My feelings are genuine. We return back to Birmingham. Eddie and I are moving out of the college campus. He has found employment dealing with furniture again. He has found us an affordable apartment. We will miss living near the college. Eddie & I visit the school regularly for eating meals in the diner. We have encountered nice compassionate people. Our son Darell was profile on the television news, pleading to the nation that if anyone see his mother & father.

Tell them to telephone his school. We would be welcome to come to Birmingham. When we arrived here, many people approach us, saying your son was on television appealing for information of your whereabouts. Eddie & I received invitations to appear at church functions, concerning Hurricane Katrina survivors. We have been ask to do television interviews. We are tired, shy and emotionally wreck. If I tried to explain the devastation of the events and aftermath of the storm and its uncertainties, I would get tangle in performances. There are still a lot of families who lived in the Gulf Coast Area is misplaced and are force to live in unfamiliar territory for obvious reasons. It is a very different way of living here. There are hills, mountains, valleys & slopes. A very clean city. This college has an excellent musical marching band. We are happy that our son is a part of their structure. I have witness him study & stay focus to earn his scholarship in music through his early years. They celebrated a homecoming festivity, while Eddie & I sat on the stoop Friday night before we were to move out. We heard the band play loudly. The students are celebrating with fireworks. The sky is lit. We could hear cheering. Darell is happy to be affiliate with these actitures. It is the Thanksgiving holiday my father-in-law Mr. George. Eddie's dad has came to town to visit us in our apartment.

Mr. George is spending quality time with his son. They miss each other & have a close relationship. Eddie's dad is like a father to me. I have been his daughter in-law for thirteen years. He act as though he is Darell's parental grandfather. He mail us uplifting gifts for holidays & special occasions. Dad always has been loving & willing to assist us in any way possible. He gave us a large sum of money to help with buying our necessity during the Hurricane Katrina saga. We had spent several Thanksgiving holiday meals together in different states. Tonight is New Year's Eve. Darell is having a party at his apartment. Eddie & I arrived before twelve o'clock. His friends are playing cards, drinking liquor, and listening to loud music. They seem to be enjoying themselves. I stirred around the apartment for awhile, talking to his guests. I retired to my son's bedroom & laid down. His parents are sleeping over night. Darell came into his room. He ask, if I am feeling alright? We talked about some events that has happen since Hurricane Katrina, devastated our home. We pray for a better New Year. I went to sleep. Early the next morning Eddie & I awaken & got dress to leave Darell's apartment. We made plans to go to the local hospital emergency room. We enter inside. Our wait is very long, all day. The doctor examines me & order specify testes. Another doctor enter into my room he introduce himself as Dr. Ray. The head surgeon of this hospital.

He explains to me. What the test showed. He elected to do surgery right away. The nurse prepped me for surgery adding medication. I was asleep immediately. When I awaken there is tubing, attach to my abdominal, connected to a wound vac machine. I was hospitalizes for thirty nine days. A very long recovery process, afterwards I am eagerly ready to go home to our apartment. Dr. Ray discharged me. I said good-bye to the hospital staff who has become my new friends here in Birmingham Alabama. My husband came to take me home. I am stirring around indoors each time that I walk to the stream door to look outside. There is a male, who is trying to get my attention. He is the nearest neighbor. Finally, he introduces himself, ask about my recovering & long stay away in the hospital. One day while I stood in the doorway, I witness this guy do something unusual. He is digging into the apartment's complex humongous trash can bin. He is dumpster diving & he is collecting garbage. He searches for electronics or scrapped iron.

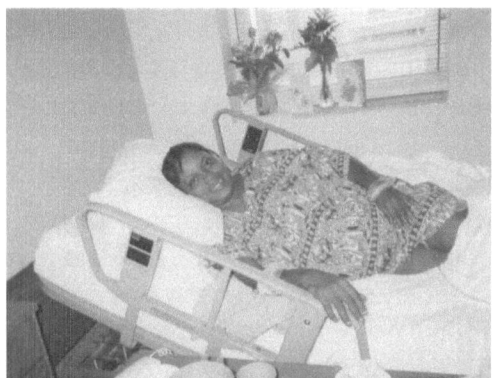

He's a fixer man. He carries junk into his apartment and allows it to pile up. The moment of truth was revealed when he moved out of his unit. Oh my God!" I have never witness this kind of a mess inside of an apartment. His trash is build up several feet off the floors, throughout each rooms. The door is jammed by garbage. There is no other entry way. Several people try to push the door open from the outside. This man lived like a pig. The Board of Health came out to his apart and evicted him. They condemned the unit for several months. He had put his neighbors, health at risk. Every morning my family smelled a file odor in our bathroom. We didn't know that it was his trash building up. We were connected wall to wall. The apartment complex owner, had to order a deep long bin to extract pounds of nasty trash. If I didn't witness this situation with my own eyes I wouldn't believe how some folks live with so much junk. He must be mentally ill. Never the less. I'm glad he and the stench is gone. I'm sure that's a permanent habit of his. Soon after this episode. I had to have another surgery. I had a lump inside my back on the lower part near my spine. Dr. Ray will be my surgeon again. I desire another doctor for this operation Dr. Ray does not like to give his patients adequate pain medications. He associates getting plenty of rest and allowing time for the body to heal is his method for recovering. I told him that pain medication is a requirement for me. I will inform him when I stop hurting. Dr. Ray is a very good surgeon. He's not a good doctor. He have bad bedside manners. He doesn't listen to his patients. The doctor is arrogant and very abusive. He believes that I am suffering from more than physical ailments. His assumption is that he met me in the emergency room under the Hurricane Katrina status. He said, I'm aggravated about my personal lost. I told him that I'm dealing with one problem at a time. I need him to treat my physical pain with medications. He & I continue to clash. I called the hospital administrator to media between he & I. I demanded more medication. I am recovering miserably. I am suicidal & overwhelm by pain. These are serious surgeries, one major one behind another. The administrator had a chat with my doctor to clear up this matter. Surely, I'm not the only patient that has complained. I reassured them that I am not a addict. There were no records of drug abuse in my blood tests. I am not self mediating in dealing with my sorrows. I'm diabetic, and having a hard time healing, it is a lengthen process. Dr. Ray removed the lump off on my back. He jokingly said, I should feel much lighter and it is non-cancerous. The nurse assisted me out of bed to walk me around the corridor she told me I'm getting discharge tomorrow. Dr. Ray has special order to give you. I told her that this surgery may take months for me to recovery from this part of my body

Chapter 4

It is three months of recovering into this New Year. It is time for me to telephone Fema (Federal Government Agency) to claim Eddie & I property settling monies. A lady representative answered the line. I gave her our disaster number and the date of Hurricane Katrina & Rita. She ask me to stay on the line. I said O.K. When she returned to the telephone, she said I must inform you that your claim has been paid out already. I shout, no way that's possible. I had been sick in the hospital for a long period of time. She said this agency, has paid your son Darell. The check went directly to him at the college. We award him the hefty benefit monies. I scream loudly, like a wounded animal, who has been caught in a trap, still alive and is being devour. She said that Darell present his I.D. picture, his & your address, telephone number & Fema application. She apologized and hung up. My antenna went on, thinking about how he could afford that nice apartment he live in on the hill. Driving a reliable radiant car, moved out his dormitory & send for Tracy & their baby from Texas State. I am sick from the shock of this news. Eddie is walking to work in all type of weather. We live in the hood, affordable housing, Darell was spending Eddie & I money as though it was his and he earn it. How darn he steal my money right from under our nose. Darell came over to our apartment late that evening. I told him what the Fema representative lady said to me. I ask him how did this happen? He said that the agency did award him our check. He had filed for himself benefits before Eddie & I came to town. He received the money in the month of December before the Christmas holidays

Darell ask me. Do I remember when he gave me at least two thousand dollars in cash? He brought me a winter jacket, and Eddie a pair sneaker, add the DVD player and you some hair products. I said yes that's where the money came from, for me to buy those items. No no no no way I shouted. You shouldn't have file before us. Darell wasn't in Hurricane Katrina. He had left home three weeks before the storm hit the city. I told him. How dare you spent our money. Eddie & I paddle our way to safety and you end up with all the money. No way. This just can't be. My mind can't comprehend this betrayal and us not getting paid. How can you do this to your own mother? I don't deserve this from you. I've been good and loving, honest and firm. I've help you walk away from the means streets of the city. I help you prepare for school. I support you, never did I put a bill in your name, hendering you from appling for personal loans & credit cards, you were able to make your own success. My family members try to tell me that Darell had gotten a windfall. They suggested the money maybe Eddie & mines. I told them, that can not be true. My son wouldn't do me anything like that. People were gossiping, saying I am foolish for allowing him to rip us off. Honestly, we are extremely hurt by his actions. We were expecting our money to help rebuild. Our needs are greatly include expensive medications, co-pay cost to see the doctors, hospital bills, clothes and a reliable car, to get around in. Eddie is furiously angry with him. He said if your son really knew you. He should have known that you would share some of that money with him. When the Fema check arrived to him at school. He should have said. "Here mom" look what Fema spent. This is from you guys property settlement. Can you share some of the money with me? That is what a loving son would have done. I am so devastated, like the time that my oldest beloved son Tori died, and I witness him laying in a coffin. I am unable to breathe in both of these situation. I could faint sitting up. Although I had not seen the check or felt the money in my hands, I had plans for that large amount of money.

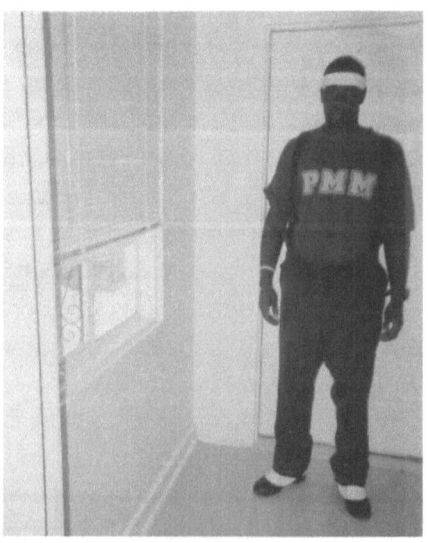

It would have last awhile for the difficult times, and our personal needs. I made several oral and written appeals to Fema/Federal Government Agency and the small business loans, the people who are involved in the decision making. Have responded saying sorry for your son misdeeds. We have paid on that claim. You need to stop, writing and calling these agencies, I am hassling them. It is in your best interest to except what has happen. I cried & cried hard not knowing how to get my needs met and help my husband out in any way. I am recovering from surgery. Every day the stress is wearing me down. I went to the closet where Darell are storing his personal belonging I have pack them up. I mean everything that is a reminder of him. After I had finish, I telephone him on his cell phone to inform him to come and get his stuff. Love doesn't live here anymore. Fools don't either. He didn't deserve me as his mother. I am withdrawing my support from him. As of us, I want him out of my apartment and my life. He had awarded himself, indulging in having a good life & time off of my husband & his mother expense. While our bills keep piling up. Darell arrived to the door. I heard him knocking. I open it up. I point at his items, all gather neatly. I witness him hauling them outside. I am still angry & my showing any emotions. I am thinking that the sooner he get out of my sight. The better I may feel. I just need quietness. All I hear is my heard pounding loudly. There is no way I can recoup my money. Darell had no money left. He had good time it away. I slammed the door behind him. Eddie is concern for my mental stability. This is a big leap for justice, against my nature of fiery. I am sitting on the sofa going over the contrast. I heard a lite tap on the door. I open it. There stood a tiny woman. She introduce herself as Ms. Winters from a well known organization for families in crisis. She said I am aware that your family needed assistance for medications & other necessities. I answer yes. I let her inside. The lady showed me her I.D. card. We both sat on the sofa. I explain what happen to my recovery funds with Darell & Fema. She heard the bitterness in my voice & my words became weaken. Ms. Winters stared at me with empathy. She announce that she is a social worker & has knowledge of being a therapist. I need both. She reach me a food card and a gift certificate. She said this is a start to lighten the load from your mind. I smile and said thank you.

She wrote down in her tablet. To visit me on a Monday of every week. She add that it is going to take a lot of willingness on my behave to help Eddie sort out this situation, to get some balance. He has been hurt also by Darell's actions. I agree with her, by nodding my head. Ms. Winters stood on her feet to exit out of the door. We shook hands. Her final words to

me. Is everything is going to be alright. You will have to give it time. After
I closed the door behind her. I thought. All is not lost. God has sent us
help. I don't feel as distraught. I can give up my idea to committed suicide.
Maybe I can live with embarrassment, paranoia & betrayal by someone who
I deeply love. I have endure bad situations before. This time remind me of
a familiar difficult period. Ms. Winters visit and therapy sessions brought
out all of my sensitive and misplaced anger that I have incurred for many
years. I realized that both of my sons manipulated our relationship. My oldest
child betrayed me in his untimely death. My youngest son for his theft. I
have to take responsibilities for putting so much store and opportunity,
allowing them to deceive me. Trust is a great weapon to misuse against the
unsuspecting person. I have created my own demons. People only do what
you allow. Counseling has freed me from guilt and finding forgiveness. I
must stand on something solid. This treatment is tapping into my deepest
depressive cycle. Surely!" there will be merit at the end of healing.

Ms. Winters organization has been very helpful. Personally, she has
given me rides to my doctor's appointment, the food stamp office, and to
the career center for placing my resume on the employment listing. The only
place I didn't have to go to is a marriage counselor. Ms. Winter suggested
that I discuss about my marriage on the last session. I said that Eddie and
I are compatible. People respect us as a inspiring couple. He respect my
mind, however difficult that maybe from time to time. He enhanced &
cultivate my thoughts by taking me places, showing me new sites. He gave
me unconditional love. I have beautiful memories of the many events in
our life. Ms. Winters smile when I spoke about the love, and many years of
marriage I have with my husband. She agree that Eddie is generally a nice
guy. He loved his family, even though it's been difficult raising my sons.
One week later Ms. Winters took me to the psychiatrist. We talk in dept
about my desire to return back home. He said I am jealous because all of
my family members has return back home. I feel powerless, have hatred, feel
trample on, abandon & detach, from losing my son's ceramics in Hurricane
Katrina. The psychiatrist said.

I judge myself on how much money I have. Not on my ability to earn
and fulfill what I need to accomplish my goals. It has been a long road to
recovery after Hurricane Katrina. We are living in a new city. We can't lose
sight about our reason for choosing Birmingham Alabama. Darell is here.
He still need guidance. He was not mentally prepared for college or to leave
home. With God's help. Eddie will restore his family back together. As we
lay in bed each night, our thoughts are, what has we done to deserve these

mishaps. The bad news continue to come. Eddie & I contemplated our options with ovation. This city & state has strong family tied. Folks from abode is not favorable some citizens, act as though they are superior in status and from another planet. There is no unity in color skin. Strangers feel no entitlement here. If a person is not affiliated with a church, school activities, athletic sports, restaurants and council town meeting popularity. You are outcast, belittle and suffer from pure boredom. Alabama State is beautiful & clean. Most city residence are snobs, bullies & common folks. We have been told to go back home to your city. Honestly! "What people haven't realized. All of this land belongs to God. We are just visitors on this earth. No one owns a spot. Shame on the men & women who are dividing & conquering space. There is enough room for others to occupy, walk about, lived in or near anyone. My family has brought flavor & character to this mix. We could live here as long as we desire.

Chapter 5

I have met Darell's new girlfriend who name is Jackie. She is a original native of Alabama. He met her at their college. I was in the hospital when he introduced her. She seemed to be very pleasant. She brought me gifts on every visit. I told her to stop spending her money on me.

I am sure that she has important things to buy herself. They seem happy together. It was only a few months when she announced that she is pregnant. This will be her first baby. She has drop out of college. No doubt, she will insist that Darell does the same. She demanded him to man up. Get a job. Be a father, no more hustling to his classes. Darell has been suspended from school for the second time. He has lost his focus. They have trade their education for parenthood. Jackie is excited about being a new mom. She is infatuated with him. She has lane, the popular, talkative, out of towner, city slicker in school. They have no plans to pursue & farther their education. I am disappointed. The telephone rang. I answer it. It is a unfamiliar male voice on the line. Jackie's uncle. He said, Jackie gave birth to a girl. I respond saying, tell her. I pray that her & the baby are well. I hung up. Soon, I smile at the notion that the baby is a girl. Days later, I received a telephone call from back home. My step-dad, Mr. Joe has suddenly died. It is a year later after my mother's death. He probably grieved himself. He & my mother spend many years together. I was eight years old when she brought him home to live with us. He was a decent man. My mother loved him. Our biology father was away in prison. When we were young, Mr. Joe step in and assist our mother in raising her three girls. Mother initial the relationship with our dad to have involvement with his children. That solution made him very happy to share & maintain a loving role. Daddy promise us, when he get release, we will have plenty of years together. Ms. Winters took me to the psychiatrist appointment on the day of Mr. Joe's funeral. Eddie & I didn't have enough money to attend the funeral back home. I would have like to pay my last respect. He deserved that from me. Mr. Joe suffered from loneliness. He battle for his life in Hurricane Katrina. Then he lost the woman he loved in the aftermath. The doctor witness the sorrow that display on my facial expression. He suggested that I disconnect with my desire for home or the guilt from not attending the services. I must live in the present moment where it's mentally safe. The doctor asked me? Haven't I realized the possibility that my family may not want me to return home? If they did, they would have sponsored me a visit on these special occasions, holidays or birthday celebrations. Ms. Winters nodded her head in agreement with him. He add families support each other in dealing with serious matters. Take your medication, sleep until your sorrows pass over. I have a prescription for Prozac & Busbar. I swallow down the pills. I slept until I settle with Mr. Joe passing away.

Today I have a doctor's appointment. Ms. Winters is giving me a ride to the hospital. It is always unpleasant to see Dr. Ray. My name is call for me to go into the examination room. He seems annoyed & visibly upset with his low tolerance feud.

The tiny Jewish lady is present with me and she is carrying her appointment tablet with her. I introduce them. I told Dr. Ray, Ms. Winters is my social worker. He responded back what do you need that for? I answer him back, by reminding him of my other issues he claims that I have. Help is here. He said you & I have a doctor & patient confidentially. I said. I've wave my right. I will allow Ms. Winters to stay & observe. Dr. Ray examines me thoroughly. He is admitting me in the hospital for the third time. My wound is not clean & healing properly. It needs to be soaked out & attach to the wound vac machine again. Early morning of the surgery, Dr. Ray entered my room. He is dress for the operation. He has a confuse glare on his face & delivering me bad news. An immediate family member has been in a serious car accident. He can't with good conscious perform my surgery. He has made preparation for his colleague to do it. Dr. Ray left out of my room. Dr Woods enter in. He tells me everything is going alone as plan. Do not be afraid. He ordered me pain medication. I went to sleep. I awaken & felt for the long heavy padded bandages that stretch from the top to the bottom. My stomach was slit in half, extremely deep. Dr. Ray returned back in a week. He & I must discuss this ugly wound. That is cut so deep near my vital organs. When the intern doctors are changing the bandages, Dr. Ray is surprise himself of how long the cut is and how deep. I am lucky to survive that surgery. I told Dr. Ray that this incision may take at least half of a year to heal in the inside. I am afraid of all of these stitches. He listen to me complain. Dr. Ray said I will keep you in the hospital a little longer for treatment. The interns doctors will teach your husband how to maintain, keeping the wound & dressing clean. He ordered me to laid still while Eddie change the bandages. When I arrived home, my husband cleaned it three times a day. Than my sister Cynthia come to visit us. We were happy she is here. I need her company & love. Darell need to talk to her to help mediate between our family breakdown. Eddie met her at the airport. I hadn't seen her since our mother's funeral. She stayed in town a couple of weeks, while vacationing from her employment. Things seem a little easier after she left for home. Ms. Winters visit again. She told me exciting news. She had knowledge that a large organization is assisting Hurricane Katrina survivors. It is call "means of recovery funds for families. I call the place for an appointment. The date of it was so far away. I hope that there were still enough money left. Eddie & I went to their office. We were escorted in by a young adult female receptionist. I am prepared & I have all our important documents, that's needed. It is establish through the paper work that Eddie is the legal person, head of household at the disaster address at the time of Hurricane Katrina in our New Orleans neighborhood area. Ms. Winters come to our regular sessions. She asked me to sat down. She is very upset. She shared with me the news that my son Darell has been awarded the Hurricane Katrina recovery funds. That particular organization allowed him to pick out an expensive car & other personal items. She add, that Eddie & I would not be receiving any money benefits. In all of the case for assistance & issuing out is. One member per household Ms. Winters gave me the name of the superior of that department. Her name is Ms. Shelly. I telephoned her immediately and explain the situation, that Darell fraudulent recieved my husband & I benefits money from Fema (Federal Government Agency) he was not the legal person. My husband & I were so astonish to prosecute him. Darell was not in the storm call Hurricane Katrina. He was away here in Birmingham Alabama. He left our city three weeks before it hit. I can prove that claim with documents, Ms. Shelly listened to me with a bias attitude saying that parents should pay for their children while they are in college. I answered her back by saying, I have. How do you think he got to college? It was my many years of planning for his future and many sacrifice from his biology father, his step-dad & from his mother. She responded back, saying moving away for school. Doesn't mean he has moved out. She is sure that he left some of his personal property at home. I told her. I can prove my husband Eddie is the man of the house at that awarded address

She better make sure that Darell proof and paper work is in order. I am furious with both of them. Darell is selfish & greedy. Ms. Shelly has complicated Eddie & I from collecting the means of recovery funds. They want to pick a fight with me. By Ms. Shelly allowing Darell to rob and cheat us again. This time I am prepared for battle. Some of us players is going down. He is my son & I must love him unconditionally. Ms. Shelly is going to wish she had never knew or heard the name Cheryl. Ms. Winters came to my house on another sessions. She told me that she has personally talk to Ms. Shelly. She has verify the situation. The recovery monies must be authorized to Mr. Edward Richardson. I told Ms. Winters that her efforts are too late. Darell is riding in his expensive car. Funded by a well known organization. Eddie & I are modify. We need the reliable car. Darell live on the college campus with friends. I told Ms. Winters that I would go through any special procedures to make things right. She gave me a toll-free number and a supervisor name to the organization and a special fraud hotline. I appreciate Ms. Winters assisting me by stirring us in that direction. I telephone Washington, D. C. Date Base. I call the fraud line, report my claim, I spoke to a supervisor explain my suspicion. I describe the event, Ms. Shelly misuse of distributing out the funds & her bias attitude of favoring my son action, against his parent's ownership. She is fully aware of his deception & disregarding the facts. Within two weeks of the charges. Ms. Shelly telephone us, offering to pay out my huge hospital bill, add money in my zero account balance to the pharmacy for medicine and two months on our rent. No money offer for Eddie's reliable car. I told Ms. Shelly no. It is too late for us to except your offer Washington D.C. Data Base will settle on the right person for this entitlement and the cash amount. They will be proceeding on with their investigation. We have a confirmation number. While battling against the organizations, Ms. Shelly & Darell, Eddie's employer telephoned him. He asked if he could come to our apartment to talk to the both of us. Eddie agreed he wonder what is this about. Mr. Clark arrived. He said Mr. & Mrs. Richardson. I have merged both of my furniture stores. I am struggling to keep this business afloat. I must lay Eddie off. He is the last man hired. Eddie & I looked at Mr. Clark in disbelief. His boss is prepared. He reached Eddie an envelope with cash money to tie him over for a short time letter of reference & termination papers. After Mr. Clark left Eddie made plans to go to the unemployment office immediately. I have plans to go to the food stamps office. This will be my fourth attempt. We always get the same worker name Ms. Kelly. She act like the food stamps belong to her. She continually turned us down, stating that Eddie, earn too much money for our household. I ask her on the last visit. How is that? Today is brand new. I am in no mood for her to reject our application. She called our name. He present her with his termination letter, Ms. Kelly ask me what is my status. I told her that I am recovering from another surgery. I raised up my blouse for her to witness my bandages. She responded. Can you get a document from your doctor regarding clearance? I boldly stated to her. I rather go to work than to go back to see that introverted doctor right now. I ask Ms. Kelly can she come up with another alternative. She said, go to the Career Center Employment Agency, apply for work. I agreed. My final words were, try not to take long issuing the food stamps please. She has a unique way of prolongation. Ms. Winters came to our regular appointment. There is much to discuss about Eddie new dilemma. She listened intensely while I explain the revelation. We were overwhelmed by the fact that it will take weeks before Eddie's unemployment checks come through. Our rent payment is nearly due. Ms. Winters offer to bring over her Sunday newspaper employment section, to assist him through his job search & food from her office pantry or give me a voucher. After she has made all of her attempt to help, she whispered to me that she is leaving the organization. That she has been employed with for many years. I badly ask her why? I assumed that Ms. Winters has been reprimand for leading me directly to the commandant personnel. I apologized for any trouble, and offer tack to her with staying with her employer. It is an attempt at kindness for all the assistance that Ms. Winters has given us. She told me to not worry about her. We have plenty of time left before her rap up date. Ms. Shelly maybe involved in this mess. She claimed that Ms. Winters is too involved with the Richardson's family, keeping friction between Darell & his mother. That is not conclusive. Both ladies are social workers and they have cross path they work for opposite, helpful, popular & outstanding organizations. Ms Shelly is taken in by Darell manipulation, milking the system of giving without compassions for others. He says it is survival skills he is utilizing. Ms. Shelly is still in her comfort zone. Every two days Eddie leave home riding his bicycle in the local area for employment. One day he rode his bike to a job site, lean it against a clear window. He went inside to fill the application out. When he witness a man has jump on the bicycle and pumping hard to get away. Eddie tried to run and give chase. He returned home angrily & told me about his bike situation. We laugh hard. It made us crave for that reliable car. The next day is my doctor appointment with the mean old Dr. Ray. Ms. Winters assist me with a ride to the hospital. She came with me into the examination room. Dr. Ray didn't rough me up, nor make nasty remarks. He shared with Ms. Winters about the first time he met me in the emergency room hospital during the Hurricane Katrina catastrophe she desire prescription pain medication. I interrupt him by saying, yes I do. My pain is aggravating from having three major surgeries, two abdominal and back sites. Dr. Ray reached me a paper stating that I can return to employment. It has been two year & six months of a recovering period. I had file for disability one year ago. I cannot withdraw my application. I have other serious health conditions that I receive treatment for. If I had a job, I am sure that it would not be waiting on me for this long period. The good news is, I am feeling much better than when I enter into this hospital. I will not have to deal with Dr. Ray snobbish remarks, and his terrible bedside manners. On our ride back home, Ms. Winters told me that today is our last day together. The days, weeks & years has pass by us quickly. I am at a loss for words. I am in deep thoughts. Should I apologize for my family situation? I could compliment Ms. Winters for being a excellent social worker, friend & therapist. I will say thank you & your organization for the assistant that were given to me & my family. She has become more than an professional assets. She, not only help me work through the unforeseen issues. She has reach into the depth & core of my soul. We arrived at my apartment. I got out of her car. Ms. Winters' final words was. I didn't dislike your son Darell. I didn't like what he done to you & Eddie. He need to face his bad deeds. Good luck with Washington D.C. I cried as I place my key inside the lock. I felt human again, out from under a deep fog inside my mind & my heart. Two weeks later Ms. Shelly telephoned me, saying to come and sign for your checks that Washington D.C Data Base has disbursed. She told me her office hours. I telephone Darell to take me there. The three of us has come face to face. Ms. Shelly immediately embraced her adoptive son. She didn't look at all like I have imagined. I said to her with dignity. I am Mrs. Richardson. I didn't look like what she has imagine either. After signing for the checks, I felt the vibes of Darell & Ms. Shelly thoughts. He received his award in cash. You are receiving your royalties in vouchers, non refundable cash, payable to the vendors. I stood up to exit her office Ms. Shelly ask me can she talk privately. Darell walk away to his car. I linger behind. She began saying how her work hour has be cut to a minimum, her seniority has been stripped. Her company has down side. There has been an investigation. She is trying to get a rise from me. All of my years of professional therapy is put to the test. I politely said to her if you are as good at your job the way you think you are?

You should not have a problem finding another one. She answered, I am a Christian woman. I said. That is good. The same merciful God that I came to know will come to your aid too. In his own time. I thought to myself now!" Go and clear out your desk. You witch. The next day is Saturday. I open the front door and witness snowflakes, falling from the sky, onto the rooftop of our apartment complex. I rush to the bedroom to alert Eddie. We put on heavy clothing. I stood outdoors, letting the flakes tap on my face. The cold & wettest add to the mix. Today I am embracing a new life, a new way of living. Darell relationship with us has gotten better. God has even the odds. We are citizen of Alabamians, neighbors, friends grandparents, family, employees, patient, author & Christians. This was a strange adventure. We have survived. We are blessed.

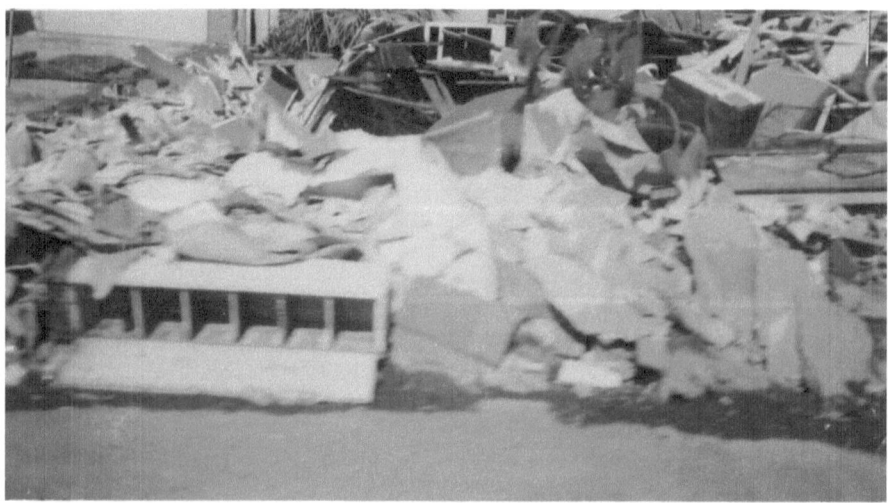

www.ingramcontent.com/pod-product-compliance
Lightning Source LLC
Chambersburg PA
CBHW061229280526
45784CB00006B/2690